Dedicated to the courage of all migrants,
cherished traditions, and the gift of family.

Illustrations and design by James Fox Rogers

when the tomatoes are ready

A short story and cookbook
by Georgia Spanos

Illustrated by James Fox Rogers

Contents

When the Tomatoes Are Ready   2

Pomodoro Pelati - peeled tomatoes   10

Passata - puréed tomatoes   12

Peperoncino Secco - dried chilli   14

Frittelle - zucchini fritters   16

Polpette di Riso - rice croquettes   18

Peperoni Arrostiti - roasted capsicums   20

Scarola - escarole w. oil, garlic & parmesan   22

Piselli e Cipolla - peas and onion   24

Pasta e Piselli - pasta and peas   26

Insalata - salad   28

Insalata di Patate - potato salad   30

Trushuni - borlotti bean soup   32

Minestra Maritata - married soup   34

Cotoletta - crumbed chicken   36

Carne alla Pizzaiola - pizza-style meat   38

Sugo Pomodoro - tomato sauce   40

Ragu - meat sauce   42

Pasta All'uovo - egg pasta   44

Gnocchi - potato pasta   46

Cannelloni Ragu - stuffed pasta   48

Lasagne Ragu - layered pasta   50

Crostoli - fried pastries   52

Cannoli - tubed custard pastries   54

Turdilli - honey balls   56

Turdilli di Vino - wine balls   58

Mutsasola - biscotti   60

Pizzelle - wafer biscuits   62

When the Tomatoes Are Ready

by Georgia Spanos

Soveria Mannelli sits on the bridge of Italy's stylish stiletto boot, nestled amidst the mountains of beautiful Calabria. It's a small town, known for its spicy salami, precious silk and chestnut trees. It's also the place Saveria Sirianni and her seven brothers and sisters call home.

When Saveria was young, her Nonna told her she had wonderful hands for kneading. It was inevitable she would become the family cook. However, chopping onions, mixing batter and shaping gnocchi proved to be a tiring task for a family of ten. What 20-year-old Saveria really needed was a job, and they were hard to find in her small town.

Each night, after the last spaghetti had been slurped and the vinos had been drained, Saveria would walk herself to the town centre to indulge in a late-night chocolate and lemon cannoli. It was on such an evening that she spotted her cousin Giuseppe standing with a very handsome young man.

'Ciao, Saveria!' Giuseppe said. *'This is Mario. He has just returned from the war and is very pleased to be home.'*

'Welcome home,' Saveria replied. *'This must be the best cannoli you've ever had,'* she joked. Mario laughed, holding a sweet, cheeky grin.

Saveria then did as every well-mannered Italian would and invited them both for dinner the following evening. *'I made fresh gnocchi this morning and there's enough to feed the town,'* she insisted.

'Si Saveria, grazie!' replied Giuseppe. *'See you tomorrow,'* he shouted as he strode charismatically down the street. Mario walked beside him, peeking back behind his shoulder at the beautiful woman he had just met.

The next day, after the sun had passed and the night had begun, Saveria waited for her guests to arrive.

'Ciao famiglia!' Giuseppe barged in, accompanied by Mario. Saveria, balancing nerves and composure, acknowledged her guests with two polite bacis on each cheek. She then ushered them in and insisted they start eating. The evening comprised laughter, passion and "saluete!" at almost every bite and consumption was, as always, at an overload.

Concentrating on the clinks of her cutlery, Saveria stayed focused. However, cheeky Mario continued to shoot flirty looks her way. He was completely absorbed by the woman before him, besotted by her beauty, intrigued by her introversion.

Saveria tried to ignore cheeky Mario all evening, but as the cannolis and espressos signalled the meal's completion, she couldn't help but surrender to her strange and unknown feelings. She looked back at the dark, handsome and very kind Mario sitting opposite her and softly smiled back at him. Their love was instant—and it was beautiful.

Saveria and Mario spent a lot of time together after the dinner. They raced to the top of mountains. They sat by the lake. They made each other clothes, food and even songs. They talked about how there was no other place more beautiful than Italy but shared the same heartbreak that it had little future for them.

Over time, they thought of ways to make a life together in Italy. Mario started building sheds for farmers while Saveria would make petticoats and silk gowns for the ladies of Soveria. After all, the town was famous for its beautiful silk—even the Pope's gown came from Soveria. But no matter how soft the silk, life in Soveria was still a struggle, and both Mario and Saveria began to lose hope in their Italian dream together. Then, one day, Mario turned to Saveria and said, *'Why don't we move to Australia? I hear the food's not quite the same, but we can make it work.'*

Saveria smiled, both happy and sad, and said yes to Mario's proposal; it seemed like the right thing to do and there were a lot of other Italians doing the same. However, the tomatoes had barely started to grow, and there was much left for her to do in Italy. So she insisted on staying, just until the tomatoes were harvested and the last jar of her perfect passata was sealed. That way, she knew her family would have supplies for the whole year, and Mario would have time to set up their life in Melbourne.

Saveria waved goodbye to Mario at the port and, as the boat moved away and he appeared smaller and smaller, she yelled, 'See you when the tomatoes are ready!'

The summer was hot, the summer was fun, but Saveria's thoughts were elsewhere. Each morning, she would race to the garden to see how the tomatoes were growing. Unusually they had not sprouted—and it was already mid-July. Saveria began to worry.

Most of her days were spent running the same track from the letterbox to the garden. She would eagerly wait to receive a letter marked with Mario's recognisable cursive writing and would then walk around the side of the house to inspect the tomato plants, sometimes even praying beside them that something would soon grow. She loved reading Mario's letters and learning of the exciting things happening in Melbourne, learning of trams and his life working at the Jam Factory. She imagined life in Australia with him. However, as the weeks went by, and the tomatoes had not come, she began to think she would never see Mario again.

Saveria eventually gave up on the tomatoes and only occasionally bothered to peek at the plants through the kitchen window. What would the Sirianni family do without their tomatoes? There would be no lasagne, no cannelloni and certainly no ragu.

Then, on a hot September afternoon, Saveria was shelling borlotti beans when a vibrant colour caught her eye through the kitchen window. She threw open the back door to discover a very fruitful—if very late—tomato plant. It was a miracle!

In no time, the Sirianni garage was filled with hundreds of cousins ready to make passata, and also to say farewell to their beloved Saveria. They boiled, peeled, cut, squashed, jarred, garnished and sealed the tomatoes without respite, even working when torches were needed to guide the process.

They made 500 bottles of passata, 100 bottles of peeled tomatoes and 20 jars of tomato skins in oil. This year's tomato day was their best yet. Saveria couldn't have dreamed of a better last night in her beautiful Soveria Mannelli with her enormous family. The next morning, Saveria waved goodbye to her family, her friends and almost the entire town as her ship headed out to sea. She promised to let them know what Australia was like.

One long, cold month passed and the boat finally reached the port in Melbourne, Australia. Saveria spotted her love, Mario, smiling joyfully and holding a strange package wrapped in newspaper. He stood patiently in a crowd of other excited men, eagerly waiting for their loves.

Saveria stepped off the boat as Mario gently led her to the edge of the pier, handing her the strange package. She unwrapped the paper to find it full of freshly fried fish and chips, an Australian specialty.

Saveria tried a piece of the tasty fish, looked around at her new home, then turned to Mario and said, 'I think my family will really like it here.'

————————————

And so they did!

It was 1950 when Mario arrived in Australia. Saveria arrived a year later. In subsequent years, all of Saveria's and Mario's brothers and sisters followed. They have lived happily in their adopted country for more than 60 years, passing down traditional family recipes from generation to generation.

Our family has always nurtured its Italian heritage and these special recipes feature at all of our family gatherings. Food is our tradition; it's what binds us. The kitchen is the place where we come together to cook and swap recipes, to share our joys and our disappointments. Even after months of travel, when I'm eager to share my adventures with Nonna, her main interest is always what I had for dinner. Food is our simple answer to all of life's queries.

Our extended families have many traditions, and I find myself committing to several family gatherings a week. No matter what the occasion—a birthday, a funeral, Easter, a graduation or just dinner—food is always the most important guest.

There's no need to come early and help prepare. Nonna cooks for days in advance. She won't let you anyway—this is her pride and joy!

After a warm-up of bread, homemade cheeses, home-cured meats, olives and my favourite—bocconcini—a large square of lasagna follows as primo piatto. Next to come are meats and sides—large pieces of beef falling apart in a rich ragu; pork cooked with olive oil, garlic, parsley and chilli; potato salad; delicious peas; and roast vegetables. All are simply cooked but are incredibly tasty.

Wine is encouraged: a large, full glass twice a day, usually red. My Nonno followed this routine his entire life, even up until his 91st birthday. He lived a long, happy and healthy life.

For us, complaining that you are full is not an option. I've found it's much easier to continue eating than to go through the *'what's wrong, are you sick?'* fiasco.

To finish, if you get there, we indulge in carefully crafted sweets and cups of strong espresso. And don't worry about going away empty-handed. Nonna will give you leftovers to last a couple of months.

———————

The idea for this book came while I was travelling around the world, making friends where so many friendships grow—over food. Fellow travellers would praise my cooking skills, amazed that I could effortlessly make fresh pasta, ragu sauce, even biscotti. I realised that not everyone eats like I do, and that with all of the homemade bread filled with fresh salami I was given as a child, I was, perhaps, quite lucky. So, I began teaching my family recipes to everyone I met and writing the recipes in my journal.

In the same journal, I would also write stories—any type of story I wished to create that day. Perhaps it was on a bus to the next town, on the beach or on days spent inside with a cup of tea, letting my brain run wild. One day, I wrote a story about my family. In particular, I wrote about my grandmother and how she met my grandfather and migrated from Italy to Australia. It was then that I discovered I was holding onto something quite incredible: my Nonna's traditional Italian recipes that flowed through her very own life story.

This book has been a special, sentimental project for me but also a challenging one—especially when it came to setting down the recipes.

Saveria does not believe in measurements you see. Quantities depend on the weather, the time of day, even the size of your hands. This proved difficult for someone trying to capture her recipes to share with the world.

My mother and I came up with a plan: as Saveria demonstrated the recipes, we secretly measured everything when she wasn't looking. Every time she turned away, we would pull out the measuring cup from our bags or quickly count the eggs. You can imagine what a long, tedious and cheeky project this was. But it also had its lighter moments, especially when Nonna caught us. We will cherish that experience forever.

This book could have been much larger. It is incredible how many dishes Saveria can make out of just a few signature Italian ingredients. It became a running joke that after years of learning Nonna's recipes, when we thought we knew her complete repertoire, she would nonchalantly serve something that we had never seen before.

'Nonna!' we would say, *'what is this recipe and why haven't you made it for us before?!'* She would always respond with an innocent grin. We started referring to the lost recipes as 'Saveria's secrets'.

When selecting recipes for this book, I chose Saveria's most tantalising, delicious dishes, the wonderful Italian home cooking that features most at our family gatherings.

My hope is that this book captures the passion, devotion and connection Italians have for food. Even after so many years in Australia, Saveria respects her family traditions. Abandoning the tomatoes was never an option, and Mario would never ask her to do such a thing.

When the Tomatoes Are Ready is not just a cookbook. It is also a life journey, a history lesson and—most important of all—a classic love story about family and food.

Buon appetito!

pomodoro pelati

peeled tomatoes

Best made in late summer in large quantities, Pomodoro Pelati is an essential pantry staple all-year-round. There's a certain comfort in having your cupboards filled with luscious tomatoes any time you need them.

Makes 6 x 340 g (12 oz) **jars**

> **4 kg** (8 lb 13 oz) **roma (plum) tomatoes**
> **6 large basil leaves**
>
> *Note: For this recipe, we use 6 x 340 g preserving jars. However, any jars you have on hand will do.*

Sterilising jars:

Preheat the oven to 140°C (275°F).

Wash the jars and lids in hot soapy water, then rinse well. Place the clean jars in a large saucepan or stockpot and fill with cold water. Place the saucepan over high heat and bring the water to a boil, then reduce to a low simmer. Boil gently for 15 minutes.

Use tongs to transfer the jars from the saucepan to a baking tray. Place the baking tray in the oven for a further 15 minutes to dry the jars.

Preparing tomatoes:

Fill a large saucepan or stockpot with water and place over high heat until the water is boiling. Add the tomatoes to the boiling water in batches.

Boil each batch for 1½–2 minutes, then transfer to a bowl of cold water.

Peel the tomato skins off immediately (they will practically slide off). Cut each tomato in half, remove the tough centres and discard.

Repeat these steps until all tomatoes are ready to be placed in jars.

Pack as many tomatoes as you can into the jars. Use a little pressure to squash them down to the bottom of the jar. The empty space will fill with tomato juice. Make sure you leave a 2 cm gap at the top.

Add 1 basil leaf to each jar and seal with lids as tightly as possible.

Cooking tomatoes:

Wrap a tablecloth around enough jars to fit in your large saucepan or stockpot, then carefully place the bundle in the saucepan. (This ensures breakage doesn't occur during boiling.)

Fill the saucepan with cold water, place over high heat and bring to the boil.

Boil for 20 minutes, then turn off the heat. This will cook the tomatoes and seal the jars.

Allow the jars to cool completely in the saucepan —if you have time, overnight is best.

Repeat these steps until all jars are sealed and ready for storage.

Store the jars in a cool, dark place, such as the pantry. They will last about 1 year, until the next tomato season comes around again. Once the jar is opened, it will keep in the refrigerator for 3–4 days.

passata

puréed tomatoes

We always look forward to tomato day in late summer, the best time of year to make this delicious sauce. Come February, dozens of cousins gather in my Zia's garage to make passata in large quantities. Think of it like salvaging the taste of summer. We all have our special jobs that have not changed for years; mine is adding a basil leaf to each jar. I like to think that I garnish the passata. The joy of cracking open a fresh bottle of passata in the middle of winter is a feeling comparable to none.

Makes 4–4.5 kg (8 lb 13 oz–9 lb 14 oz)

8 kg (17 lb 10 oz) **tomatoes**
a few good pinches of salt
1 large bunch of basil, about 60 g (2 oz)

Equipment:
preserving jars for bottling (any type, any shape)
food mill
ladle & jug

Note: If you prefer to make a smaller amount, 2 kg of tomatoes will make 1–1½ kg passata

Directions:

Sterilise the jars (see pg. 10).

Wash the tomatoes, cut them in half and remove the tough bits from the centre.

Half-fill a very large saucepan or stockpot with water and bring to the boil, then reduce the heat to a low simmer.

Add all the tomatoes and cook over medium heat for 1½ hours, stirring from time to time.

Add a few good pinches of salt.

Turn off the heat and allow the tomatoes to cool for 15 minutes.

Working in batches, process the tomatoes through the food mill, catching the passata in a large jug.

Run the leftover tomatoes through the food mill a few more times to ensure all juice has been extracted.

Use a ladle and a funnel to fill the jars with passata, leaving a 2 cm (¾ in) gap at the top.

Add 1 large basil leaf to each jar.

Seal the jars (see pg. 10) and store them in a cool, dark place, such as the pantry. They will last about 1 year, until the next tomato season comes around again. Once the jar is opened, it will keep in the refrigerator for 3–4 days.

peperoncino secco

dried chilli

As a child, I called this a chilli necklace. You would often catch me running around Nonna's house with this draped around my neck, feeling very fancy. Not only does it bring colour and character to your kitchen, but it also adds bite to any dish.

Makes 30 g (1 oz) **dried chilli**

200 g (7 oz) **baby chillies, very hot**

Equipment:
needle
polyester thread
jar (any shape, any size)

Note: The needle should have a large enough eye for the string. The needle needs to be thick enough to press through the chilli, yet not so thick that it will break the chilli stem.

Directions:

Thread the string through the needle's eye.
Use enough thread to join the chillies together with enough excess thread for hanging.

Thread the chillies together at the tip of the chilli's body, just below the stem—the hardest part of the chilli.

Push the chillies down the thread one by one when threading, meeting at the end of the thread.

Once you have threaded all the chillies together, cut the end of the thread off and tie both loose ends together.

Find a cool, dry and well-ventilated area in your house and hang the chillies to dry.

The time the chillies take to dry out will depend on the temperature, which varies for each home. However, they usually take around 3 weeks to 1 month. You will know when the chillies are dried as they will shrivel up and lose some colour. At this point, take the chillies down.

Remove the stems of each chilli and discard. Transfer the chillies to a tray.

Place the tray in the sun for a few days to extract the rest of the moisture from the chillies.

After the chillies have dried in the sun, wrap them in a tea towel (dish towel) and begin to bang the tea towel with a rolling pin or meat mallet. Bang the towel until the chillies are decently crushed and turned to flakes. (You could also use a coffee grinder, if you have one.)

Pour the flakes in your jar and seal with a lid as tight as you can. Store in a dark, cool place (such as the pantry). These can be stored for years. You can tell when the flakes are too old to use as they will grow mouldy.

frittelle

zucchini fritters

Zucchini plants are just as prominent in our garden as tomatoes or basil. They are essential in Italian cooking together with the gorgeous flowers that grow with them. The bright orange petals of the zucchini flowers, which are thrown into the batter, create a beautiful touch to these little bundles. Enjoy while hot and crispy, but be careful. When we were growing up, we would burn our mouths, as we were too eager to let them cool down.

Makes 30–40

1 kg (2 lb 3 oz) **zucchini** (courgettes), **grated**

4–5 zucchini flowers, coarsely chopped

2 large eggs

100 g (3½ oz / 1 cup) **grated parmesan**

2 good pinches of salt

150 g (5½ oz / 1 cup) **plain** (all-purpose) **flour**

35 g (1¼ oz / ¼ cup) **self-raising flour**

vegetable oil, for frying

Directions:

In a bowl, combine the zucchini, zucchini flowers, eggs, parmesan and salt. Mix thoroughly.

Gradually add flour to the mixture, handful by handful, while mixing the ingredients together.

Pour a thick layer of vegetable oil into a large frying pan (enough for shallow-to-medium frying) and place over medium heat.

Test if the oil is hot enough by dropping a small amount of mixture into the oil. If the mixture starts to fry immediately, the oil is ready. The oil must be very hot for the fritelle to crisp.

Drop generous tablespoons of mixture into the oil and flatten slightly with the back of a spoon.

Saveria Tip: As you get to the end of your mixture, you may end up with a bit of excess zucchini liquid. At this point, throw in a handful of plain flour and combine. This will bring the mixture back to a good consistency.

Fry the fritelle for 1 minute each side or until they brown and crisp. Once fried, transfer the fritelles to a paper towel to drain.

These can be served as an appetiser or for breakfast. They are best eaten while hot and crispy.

Leftovers can be refrigerated in an airtight container for up to 3–4 days.

polpette di riso

rice croquettes

Ever cooked too much rice or risotto? Well, simply put the extra rice in the fridge and, the next day, convert it into these delicious croquettes. The great thing about this dish is it can also be used as the base for arancini balls. Simply wrap your arancini filling with this mixture, roll in breadcrumbs and fry to a crisp.

Makes 75–80

500 g (1 lb 2 oz / 2¼ cups) **short-grain rice**
1 large all-purpose potato
100 g (3½ oz / 1 cup) **grated parmesan**
3 large eggs
5 tbsp. flat-leaf (Italian) **parsley, finely chopped**
50 g (1¾ oz / 1/2 cup) **dried breadcrumbs**
3 good pinches of salt
1 large garlic clove, finely chopped
vegetable oil for frying
olive oil to coat hands

Equipment:
potato ricer

Directions:

Fill a large saucepan with cold water.
Add the rice and bring to a boil, then reduce the heat and simmer for 20 minutes.

Drain the rice and cool completely; refrigerate if need be.

Saveria Tip: It's best to cook the rice the night before and refrigerate until the following day. This is so the rice is well drained and cool. If the rice holds heat, it will cook the egg and alter the taste.

Fill a separate small saucepan with enough cold water to almost fill the pot, then add the potato with its skin on. Bring the water to a boil, then reduce the heat and cook the potato for 30–40 minutes, until soft.

Immediately slide the potato skin off—it will be hot so hold the potato in a clean tea towel (dish towel) and, using your other hand, remove the skin.

Pass the potato through a potato ricer and into a large bowl. Stir in the rice, parmesan, eggs, parsley, garlic, breadcrumbs and salt, and combine well.

Using your hands, shape the rice mixture into croquette logs—about 2 x 6 cm (¾ x 2 ½ inches).

Saveria Tip: Cover your hands with olive oil for ease when rolling the croquettes. This will prevent the rice from sticking to your hands while also helping the croquettes to hold their shape.

Heat a large frying pan with a thick layer of vegetable oil (enough for deep frying) over medium heat. The oil must be very hot to avoid the croquettes absorbing too much of it. Test if the oil is hot enough by dropping in a small amount of mixture. If the rice starts to fry immediately, the oil is ready.

Fry the croquettes in small batches a few at a time. Make sure there is adequate space around them so you can flip them without touching the others. (If there are too many in the pan, the oil will cool down, the croquettes will take longer to crisp, and they may go soggy.) Turn often until they are crisp and golden, and float to the top of the oil (about 3–4 minutes).

Transfer to paper towel to drain.

These are perfect when accompanied with olives, cheeses, cured meats and other selections on an antipasto-style platter.

peperoni arrostiti

roasted capsicums (peppers)

These beautiful peppers are seen everywhere in Italy, in many different styles and forms. They are as welcome on an antipasto platter as in a salad or a pasta sauce. They're also delicious when fried with garlic and olive oil and served on good quality fresh bread.

Makes 2–2½ cups, approx. 550 g (1 lb 3 oz)

1.5 kg (3 lb 5 oz) **red capsicums** (peppers)
good pinch of salt
125 ml (4 fl oz / 1/2 cup) **extra virgin olive oil**
2 garlic cloves, halved (optional)
2 handfuls flat-leaf (Italian) **parsley, coarsely chopped** (optional)

Equipment:
clear plastic bag

Directions:

Preheat the oven to 170°C (340°F).

Wash the capsicums, then place them on a baking tray lined with foil. Place the tray in the oven and cook for 1 hour, turning the capsicums over after 30 minutes. Your capsicums should become dark and charred, and their skins will loosen.

Saveria Tip: If you pinch the capsicums and their skins easily detach, they are ready. If you find it hard to pinch their skins, they will need more time in the oven.

Transfer the capsicums from the oven directly into a plastic bag. Tie the bag shut and allow them to steam for 30 minutes.

Remove the capsicums from the bag (you may want to wear gloves as they will be hot) and slide off their skins.

Tear them lengthways into decent-sized strips, while making sure you remove the seeds and stem.

Put the capsicum strips in a bowl, add salt and coat with the extra virgin olive oil. If you would like more flavour, add 2 halved garlic cloves and 2 handfuls of chopped flat-leaf parsley. Combine well.

These are best eaten fresh. However, they can be stored in jars sealed with lids, and kept in a cool, dark place for 3–4 months. Once the jars are opened, the contents should be refrigerated and eaten within 1–2 weeks.

scarola

escarole with oil, garlic & parmesan

Escarole, or 'Scarola' as Nonna would call this, is a variety of endive with a slightly bitter taste, and, to us, the tastiest green in the garden. Scarola is perfect when added to soups, used as pizza toppings, added to vegetables or simply enjoyed on its own. In this recipe, I prepare Nonna's classic escarole with oil, garlic and parmesan.

Serves 2–3 as a side dish

- **2 bunches scarola lettuce** (escarole or endive lettuce)**, heads cut off and coarsely chopped**
- **80 ml** (2½ fl oz / ⅓ cup) **olive oil**
- **4 garlic cloves, halved**
- **good pinch of salt**
- **50 g** (1¾ oz / ½ cup) **grated parmesan** (or more if you prefer)

Directions:

Wash the lettuce well, then dry.

Pour water into a large saucepan until it's three-quarters full and bring to a boil. Add the lettuce and blanch for 2–3 minutes. Drain the lettuce.

In a large frying pan, heat the olive oil over medium heat. Add the garlic and fry for approximately 2 minutes to soften (do not brown).

Add the lettuce one handful at a time and gently stir through the olive oil and garlic. Cover and cook for 3–5 minutes.

Transfer to a serving dish, season with salt and top with parmesan cheese.

Note: Scarola is delicious when combined with cooked smashed potatoes and lots of olive oil.

For this amount of scarola, use 2 all-purpose potatoes and 60 ml (2 fl oz / ¼ cup) good quality olive oil. Boil the potatoes with the skins on until soft. Remove the skins, smash the potatoes with a fork and stir through the olive oil and the scarola. It makes a perfect side dish.

Scarola is also particularly tasty mixed with beans.

piselli e cipolla

peas and onion

I promise these will be the tastiest peas you have ever had, and you will never look at peas the same way again! By simply adding the sweet taste of fried onions, you liven up simple greens creating an impressive dish rich in flavour.

Serves 4 as a side dish

3 tbsp. olive oil

1 brown onion, diced

500 g (1 lb 2 oz / 3¼ cups) **peas** (fresh or frozen)

125 ml (4 fl oz / ½ cup) **hot water**

good pinch of salt

Directions:

Heat the oil in a saucepan over medium heat and fry the onion for about 3–4 minutes until soft (do not brown).

Add the peas along with the hot water and salt. Cover and cook for 15–20 minutes, stirring occasionally to stop the onion and peas from sticking to the bottom.

If the lid is rattling and the saucepan is too hot, crack the lid open (half on/half off) and continue cooking.

Serve hot with the gorgeous oniony liquid, which keeps the peas soft and moist.

pasta e piselli

pasta and peas

This recipe represents true Calabrian cooking. It's the perfect example of how you can use a few basic ingredients to create perfection. By simply adding pastina to the piselli and topping with lots of parmesan cheese, you transform a side dish into tasty pasta. My friends say this is their favourite recipe in the book.

Serves 4

175 g (6 oz) **ditali pastina**

500 g (1 lb 2 oz) **piselli e cipolla** (pg. 24)

grated parmesan, to serve

peperoncino secco (pg. 20)**, to serve** (optional)

Directions:

In a medium saucepan, cook the pastina in boiling salted water uncovered until al dente (about 8–10 minutes). Drain the pasta.

Put the pastina back in the saucepan and add the onion peas. Toss and combine.

Transfer to serving bowls and top with generous amounts of grated parmesan and dried chilli if you like heat.

insalata

salad

This is the only salad ever served to us by our Nonna. A simple, but perfect, complement to any big meal. There's something so refreshing about this salad—perhaps it's the fresh lettuce or the classic Calabrian dressing of olive oil, apple cider vinegar and oregano. Enjoy this salad with any dish.

Serves 4 as a side dish

½ iceberg lettuce

3 tomatoes, cut into wedges

1 cucumber, peeled and sliced

100 ml (3½ fl oz) **extra virgin olive oil**

80 ml (2½ fl oz / ⅓ cup) **apple cider vinegar**

good pinch of salt

2 good pinches of dried oregano

Directions:

Wash the lettuce and gently tear it into smaller pieces for a salad.

Add the tomato and cucumber.

Add olive oil, apple cider vinegar, salt and oregano.

Toss and combine.

insalata di patate

potato salad

This is Mario's signature dish. He was always in charge of cooking the Insalata di Patate at every family gathering, and no one quite made it like he did. The cold potatoes and tang of the apple cider vinegar dance perfectly together, and, with the freshness of Italian parsley, this dish is worth applauding.

Serves 4-5 as a side dish

1 kg (2 lb 3 oz) **all-purpose potatoes** (such as the pink-skinned desiree)

½ white onion, diced

4 tbsp. flat-leaf (Italian) **parsley, finely chopped**

100 ml (3½ fl oz) **apple cider vinegar**

100–120 ml (3½–4 fl oz) **extra virgin olive oil**

good pinch of salt

Directions:

Wash the potatoes and put them in a large saucepan (whole, skins on) filled with cold water.

Place the lid on the saucepan and bring the water to a boil over medium heat.

Once the water has boiled, cook the potatoes for approximately 30–40 minutes or until they are tender to soft. Ensure the potatoes are always completely covered with water while boiling.

Saveria Tip: It is important not to overcook the potatoes. Otherwise, they will absorb too much water and start to crumble. If this occurs, the dressing will soak into the potatoes rather than coat them.

Drain the potatoes. Cool completely in the refrigerator for 30 minutes or, if you have time, refrigerate overnight.

Once cooled, carefully remove the potato skins. Cut the potatoes into a combination of quarters and halves—then transfer to a serving bowl.

Add the onion, parsley, apple cider vinegar, olive oil and salt to the bowl.

Toss and combine.

trushuni

borlotti bean soup

Borlotti beans are certainly the most fashionable bean in the garden with their beige pods and magenta streaks. They have a wonderfully nutty flavour reminiscent of chestnuts and are essential in Italian minestrone. They're also perfect in sauces, stews and salads. This dish is very rustic, wholesome and best served up with crusty bread on a cold winter's day.

Serves 4-5

- 4 celery stalks, chopped
- ½ brown onion, diced
- 3 tbsp. flat-leaf (Italian) parsley, coarsely chopped
- 2 tbsp. basil, coarsely chopped
- 1 jar pomodoro pelati (pg. 10), chopped a few times
- 3 tbsp. olive oil
- 1 kg (2 lb 3 oz) fresh borlotti beans
- or 400 g (14 oz) dried borlotti beans
- good pinch of salt
- grated parmesan, to serve

Directions:

Fill a medium saucepan with enough water to almost fill the pot. Bring the water to a boil, then reduce the heat to a low simmer.

Add the celery, onion, parsley, basil and a jar of tomatoes. Cover and cook for 1 hour, adding the olive oil after 30 minutes.

While the soup is cooking, prepare the fresh borlotti beans. Shell the borlotti beans from their pods. Place the beans in a saucepan full of cold water and bring to a boil. Once the water has boiled, cover and cook for 5 minutes.

Drain the dark water from the beans and replace immediately with fresh hot water.

Cook for a further 30–40 minutes or until the beans are soft. Drain the beans.

Once the vegetable soup is ready, add the borlotti beans and a good pinch of salt.

Transfer the soup to a serving bowl and scatter lots of grated parmesan cheese on top.

Note: If using dried borlotti beans, you'll need to soak them in advance. In a bowl, completely cover the beans with cold water and leave to soak overnight. In the morning, replace the water with clean hot water and boil in a saucepan for around 5 minutes. Replace the water with clean hot water again, then place the saucepan back on the stove to cook for around 1½ hours until the beans are soft. Drain the beans.

minestra maritata

married soup

Just one glance at this dish, which is more like artwork than soup, and you can see the love and devotion that has gone into it. Minestra Maritata, or 'Married Soup', is actually a reference to how the chicken, vegetables and tiny meatballs marry well together. Saveria will feed this to you if you are feeling under the weather.

Serves 4-5

Soup:

1 kg (2 lb 3 oz) **chicken**

1 x 340 g (12 oz) **jar pomodoro pelati** (pg. 10)

6 celery stalks, chopped 5 mm (¼ inch) **thick**

4 carrots, peeled and chopped 5 mm (¼ inch) **thick**

½ brown onion, diced

3 large handfuls flat-leaf (Italian) **parsley, coarsely chopped**

2 good pinches of salt

100 g (3½ oz / ½ cup) **pastina**

Meatballs:

500 g (1 lb 2 oz) **minced** (ground) **beef**

70 g (2½ oz / ¾ cup) **grated parmesan**

3 tbsp. finely chopped flat-leaf (Italian) **parsley**

2 large garlic cloves, finely chopped

2 large eggs

good pinch of salt

2 slices of white bread

60 ml (2 fl oz / ¼ cup) **milk**

olive oil, for frying

To serve:

grated parmesan

Directions:

To make the soup, remove the skin from the chicken, then place the whole bird in a large saucepan along with enough water to almost fill the pot (the chicken must be completely covered with water). Bring the water to the boil, then reduce the heat to a lower simmer.

Cover and cook for 3 hours, adding the vegetables (tomato, celery, carrots, onion, parsley) and salt after 30 minutes. Skim the fat that will rise to the surface every 15 minutes or so throughout cooking.

Meanwhile, for the meatballs, combine the beef, parmesan, parsley, garlic, eggs and salt in a bowl.

Soak the sliced bread in the milk. Using your hands, squeeze the milk from the slices and tear them roughly a few times. Add the torn bread to the mixture (this is to soften the meatballs). Gently work the mixture together to combine the ingredients. Using your hands, roll the mixture into small balls —about 2.5 cm (1 in) across.

In a large frying pan, heat a layer of olive oil (enough for shallow frying) over medium heat.

Working in batches, fry the meatballs until they are browned on all sides and completely cooked through (approximately 15 minutes).

Once the soup is ready, turn off the heat and remove the chicken from the soup and place on a working surface.

Debone the chicken (you may want to wear gloves or use tongs as the chicken will be hot) and discard the bones. Tear the chicken meat into decent-sized pieces and place back in the soup.

In a separate saucepan, cook the pastina in boiling salted water until al dente (6–8 minutes, depending on the pastina used).

Fill each bowl with chicken soup, 4–5 meatballs, pastina and lots of grated parmesan.

cotoletta

crumbed chicken

Cotoletta is my favourite way to enjoy chicken. My mother remembers this in her lunch every day at school, accompanied with a thick slice of pasta dura bread. This recipe can be used for any type of meat—veal is particularly good.

Makes 15-20

800 g (1 lb 12 oz) **chicken breasts** (or try any other meat you'd like)

75 g (2¾ oz / ½ cup) **plain flour**

3 large **eggs**, beaten

2 tbsp. **milk**

1 large **garlic** clove, finely chopped

2 tbsp. finely chopped flat-leaf (Italian) **parsley**

good pinch of **salt**

200 g (7 oz / 2 cups) **breadcrumbs**

vegetable oil, for frying

2 **lemons**, cut into wedges, to serve

Equipment:

meat tenderiser

clear plastic bag

Directions:

Trim the skin and fat from the chicken breasts. Slice each breast through its middle into fillets (about four times), then place the fillets in a clear plastic bag.

Using a meat tenderiser, beat the bag until the fillets are 5 mm (¼ inch) thick. This will tenderise the chicken.

Cut the fillets into smaller pieces if necessary.

Prepare three plates:

1. Flour
2. A mixture of eggs, milk, garlic, parsley and salt
3. Breadcrumbs

Handle the chicken breast by pinching its corner and moving it along each plate.

Coat both sides in flour, dip in the egg mixture and then bury in breadcrumbs. Press the crumbs into the fillets with your fingertips.

Continue this process until you have crumbed all chicken breasts then refrigerate for 1 hour.

After the hour, heat a large frying pan with a moderate layer of vegetable oil (enough for shallow frying) over medium heat.

Once the oil is very hot, fry each fillet until brown, cooked through and crispy (about 4–5 minutes each side).

Transfer the fillets to a paper towel to drain.

Serve with warmed lemon wedges.

carne alla pizzaiola

pizza-style meat

Carne alla Pizzaiola (literally translated to Pizza-Style Meat) is an old recipe traditional to the pizza maker's wife. Using a piece of good quality meat, she would use the pizza ingredients from the shop, such as ripened tomato and oregano, to slow-cook this dish together. Once cooked, you can serve the meat with slices of fresh bread, in a ciabatta roll to soak up the beautiful juices or Saveria-style with sides of piselli, insalate di patate or insalata.

Serves 2

500 g (1 lb 2 oz) **scotch fillet**

3 tbsp. **olive oil**

2 large **garlic cloves**, halved

4 ripened medium **truss tomatoes**, sliced

5 flat-leaf (Italian) **parsley sprigs**

good pinch of salt

60 ml (2 fl oz / ¼ cup) **hot water**

good pinch of dried oregano

To serve:

slices of good quality fresh bread

or ciabatta rolls

piselli e cipolla (pg. 24)

insalate di patate (pg. 30)

insalata (pg. 28)

Directions:

Trim any fat from the meat.

Heat the oil in a large frying pan over medium heat for a minute or so, then add the fillet and brown for 3–5 minutes on each side.

Add the garlic to the pan and fry for 1 minute to soften (do not brown).

Place the tomatoes on top of the meat along with the parsley and salt. Pour the hot water into the pan.

Reduce the heat to low, then cover and cook for approximately 30 minutes or until the meat is very soft and tender.

Add the oregano in the last 10 minutes of cooking.

Saveria Tip: If there appears to be too much liquid in the pan, remove the lid while cooking and let liquid evaporate.

Serve the fillet whole on a plate with the cooked tomatoes and beautiful juices on top of the meat. Accompany with a few sides: perhaps piselli e cippola, insalate di patate or insalata.

Alternatively, for a lunch option, place the meat and its juices inside a fresh baguette. The beautiful tomato juices will ooze out with every bite—delicious!

sugo pomodoro

tomato sauce

A good sauce should never be cooked quickly. Even this staple needs at least 45 minutes to become a sauce. Nonna cooks this Italian classic for us when we feel like a light tomato pasta rather than a heavy ragu.

Serves 4-5

- 80 ml (2½ fl oz / ⅓ cup) **olive oil**
- 1 **garlic clove**, halved
- ½ medium **brown onion**, diced
- 2 x 340 g (12 oz) **jars pomodoro pelati** (pg. 10)
- 1 x 650 g (1 lb 7 oz) **jar passata** (pg. 12)
- 6 large **basil leaves**, torn a few times
- 3 tbsp. chopped flat-leaf (Italian) **parsley**
- good pinch of **salt**

To serve:

- **fresh tagliatelle** (pg. 44) **or gnocchi** (pg. 46)
- grated **parmesan**
- **peperoncino secco** (pg. 20) (optional)

Directions:

Heat the olive oil in a large saucepan over medium heat. Fry the garlic and onion for 2 minutes to soften (do not brown).

Add the peeled tomatoes, passata, basil, parsley and salt.

Cover and cook on a low simmer for 45 minutes, stirring from time to time.

After 45 minutes, if the sauce is yet to come together and thicken, remove the lid to evaporate the excess liquid and continue cooking. Cook until the sauce is thick.

Serve with fresh pasta (gnocchi is particularly good), lots of grated parmesan cheese and dried chilli (if you like a bit of heat).

ragu

meat sauce

The journey of slow-cooking ragu is special and should be cherished. It brings the smells of Italy into the house, filling the air with delicious aromas. I like to craft my days at home around cooking this dish. Perhaps I'm writing, calling family or friends, or simply taking a step back to enjoy time with myself while I watch the beautiful ragu come together.

Serves 4-5

1 kg (2 lb 3 oz) **rump beef steak**

80 ml (2½ fl oz / ⅓ cup) **olive oil**

2 large **garlic cloves, halved**

½ **brown onion, diced**

2 x 340 g (12 oz) **jars pomodoro pelati** (pg. 10)

1 x 650 g (1 lb 7 oz) **jar passata** (pg. 12)

6 large **basil leaves, torn a few times**

3 tbsp. **flat-leaf parsley, coarsely chopped**

2 good pinches of **salt**

To serve:

fresh tagliatelle (pg. 44) **or gnocchi** (pg. 46)

grated parmesan

Directions:

Pat the beef dry with paper towels to remove the excess liquid.

Trim the fat from the meat and discard. Cut the meat into decent-size pieces—about 2.5 x 3 cm (1 x 1¼ inches).

In a large saucepan, heat the olive oil over medium heat, then add the garlic and onion. Fry the garlic and onion for 2 minutes until soft (do not brown).

Add the meat chunks and brown for approximately 15 minutes, stirring every minute or so.

Add the peeled tomatoes and tomato passata along with 125 ml (4 fl oz / ½ cup) of water (which can be obtained by filling the empty tomato jars with water). Add the basil leaves and parsley.

Bring the sauce to the boil, and then reduce the heat to a low simmer. Cover and cook the sauce for 3–3½ hours, stirring from time to time. Add salt in the last hour of cooking.

You will know when your sauce is ready as the meat will be very tender and soft and will fall apart at the touch.

Serve with fresh tagliatelle or gnocchi and lots of grated parmesan.

pasta all'uovo

egg pasta

Everyone should know how to make fresh pasta. It's surprisingly easy and requires few ingredients and just a little effort. Fresh pasta is delicate and tender and tastes completely different to dried pasta from the supermarket. Saveria's kitchen table would often be covered in huge sheets of pasta dough eagerly waiting to be cut. Don't rush out and buy a pasta machine—our secret is that you don't need one.

Serves 6

> **6 large eggs**
> **good pinch of salt**
> **500 g** (1 lb 2 oz / 3⅓ cups) (00) **flour, sifted**
>
> Equipment:
> **rolling pin**
>
> To serve:
> **6 cups ragu** (pg. 42)
> **grated parmesan**
> **peperoncino secco** (pg. 20)

Note: This pasta can be shaped to any pasta you desire. However, in this recipe we will make tagliatelle, the most commonly made pasta in our family.

Directions:

Combine the eggs and salt in a bowl and mix with a fork for 30 seconds.

Gradually add the sifted flour while mixing the ingredients together. Continue until all the flour is combined. Your mixture should now hold together yet not be sticky.

Transfer the mixture to a lightly floured working surface and knead the dough (about 5–10 min).

Saveria Tip: The best way to knead is to use the bottom palm of your hand to push the dough away from you. Quarter-turn the dough and repeat this step until the dough is smooth and pliable. If the dough sticks to your hands while kneading, add a little more flour.

Roll out the dough until at least 1–2 mm thin.

Saveria Tip: Dust the top of your mixture with flour and wrap the edge of your dough around the rolling pin. Using your fingertips, apply a small amount of pressure to the dough while simultaneously rolling the dough outwards along the stick. This will stretch it lengthways. Do this on each corner of the dough.

Let the dough rest for 30 minutes—go do your banking, hang up some washing or do some gardening.

After 30 minutes, it's time to cut the pasta. Fold the mixture 3–4 times over lengthways. Using a sharp knife, cut the pasta into 8 mm (3/8 inch) tagliatelle pasta strips. (However, don't put any pressure on the dough or the layers will stick together.)

Bounce the pasta strips in your hands, which will loosen the layers into tagliatelle pasta.

Dust the pasta with flour and lay out on a clean tea towel (dish towel) to dry for 10 minutes.

Note that you can use this recipe to make any pasta shape you desire. If not cooking immediately, cover with plastic wrap and store in the refrigerator for later use. It will keep for 1–2 days.

When ready to cook, place the pasta in boiling salted water and cook until al dente (about 2–3 minutes).

Transfer to a serving bowl with ragu sauce, lots of grated parmesan and dried chilli (if you like the heat).

gnocchi

potato pasta

These soft, delicate potato pillows epitomise comfort. The success of this dish largely depends on how you treat them—be gentle and methodical, and craft the gnocchi pieces with complete and utter care. Gnocchi masters respect the dough and try to use as little flour as possible.

Serves 6-8

2 kg (4 lb 6 oz) **all-purpose potatoes**
2 **large eggs, beaten**
good pinch of salt
300 g (10½ oz / 2 cups) **plain** (all-purpose) **flour**

Equipment:
potato ricer

To serve:
6-8 cups sugo pomodoro (150g per cup) (pg. 40)
or ragu (200g per cup) (pg. 42)
freshly grated parmesan

Directions:

In a large saucepan, cover the potatoes (whole, skins on) with cold water and bring the water to a boil over high heat. Reduce the heat to a low simmer and cook the potatoes until soft, approximately 30–40 minutes.

Test if the potatoes are ready by pushing a fork or knife through their centre. This requires a small amount of pressure to initially pierce the potato. This should indicate if the potato is perfectly cooked and not too soft.
Drain the potatoes and cool for a few minutes

Saveria Tip: If you cook the potatoes for too long, they will absorb too much water and require more flour. This is not ideal, as we want the gnocchi to use as little flour as possible to be light and delicate.

Peel off the potato skins. The potatoes will be hot so consider wearing gloves or hold potatoes in a clean tea towel (dish towel).

Cut the potatoes into quarters and pass them through a potato ricer into a large bowl. Add the eggs and salt to the bowl and work the ingredients together with your hands.

Transfer the gnocchi mixture to a flat working surface lightly dusted with flour.

Gradually add small amounts of flour while kneading the ingredients together. Perfect gnocchi dough will hold together and not be sticky. If you get to this point and have leftover flour, it's fine to leave out the rest—you do not need to use anymore.

Once your dough has reached the right consistency, gently knead for 5 minutes.

Test your gnocchi by cutting a small piece from the mixture and cooking it in boiling salted water until it rises to the top of the water.

Taste the gnocchi—if it is sticky, the dough may need more flour. Cut the dough into portions and roll these portions into thumb size logs. Cut the logs into small gnocchi pieces, 2 cm (¾ inch) in length.

Shape the gnocchi pieces. In one fast sharp movement, use your index finger to apply a small amount of pressure to the middle of each gnocchi piece while simultaneously rolling your finger down and off the pieces towards yourself. The result will be a small dint-like pocket in the dough in which the sauce will sit.

Cook the gnocchi in boiling salted water until the gnocchi rise to the top of the water (1–2 minutes). Use a slotted spoon to gently transfer the gnocchi to a serving plate, then top with the sauce (ragu or pomodoro) and parmesan.

Gnocchi is best served with lots of sauce and lots of cheese. Place the gnocchi into the serving bowls, then fill each bowl three-quarters full of sauce and add generous amounts of grated parmesan.

cannelloni ragu
stuffed pasta

It's quite impressive how many ways Italians can transform pasta—different shapes, different sizes, different cooking methods. Baking is just one of them. There is something truly wonderful about putting a tray of cute neatly-lined homemade cannelloni in the oven. In my family, this dish is made on special occasions as it takes some effort, but each bite certainly makes it worthwhile.

Serves 6-8

Meat filling:
500 g (1 lb 2 oz) **minced** (ground) **beef**
3 tbsp. ragu (pg. 42)
95 g (3¼ oz / 1 cup) **freshly grated parmesan**
3 large eggs
2 tbsp. flat-leaf parsley, finely chopped
1 large garlic clove, finely chopped
good pinch of salt
2 slices of bread
60 ml (2 fl oz / ¼ cup) **milk**

Cannelloni:
pasta all'uovo (pg. 44)
or 250 g (9 oz) **store-bought cannelloni tubes**

Sauce:
4 cups ragu (pg. 42)
250 ml (8½ fl oz / 1 cup) **boiling water**
45 g (1½ oz / ½ cup) **freshly grated parmesan, to top** (or more if you prefer)

Equipment:
baking dish, approximately 20 x 30cm (8 x 12 in.)

Directions:

Preheat the oven to 200°C (400°F).

For the meat filling, combine the meat, ragu, parmesan, eggs, parsley, garlic and salt and mix with a fork.

Soak the bread in the milk. Use your hands to squeeze the milk from the slices. Tear the slices a few times, then add them to the mixture.

Use your hands to gently work the ingredients together.

If you are rolling your own cannelloni, follow the steps for the pasta all'uovo recipe (pg. 44) until you roll the dough out to 1–2 mm thin, and it has rested for 30 minutes.

After the dough has rested, cut into lasagne sheets/shapes—10 x 15 cm (4 x 6 in) rectangles. Cook your pasta sheets in a saucepan of boiling salted water until al dente (2–3 minutes for fresh pasta; 8–10 minutes for dry pasta), then directly transfer to a bowl of cold water.

Working with one sheet at a time, take the lasagne sheets from the bowl and immediately lay them on a flat clean surface. Cut each lasagne sheet in half and spoon a line of the meat filling onto each sheet (lengthways).

Roll into tubes, just making the ends meet—do not have too much overlap.

If using store-bought cannelloni tubes, fill the tubes with the meat mixture using your hands or the back of a spoon. Ensure you fill the tubes right to their edge. Transfer all cannelloni tubes to a baking dish, neatly lining them beside each other.

Pour the ragu sauce over the cannelloni tubes, then pour over the boiling water and top with parmesan cheese.

Cover with foil and cook in the oven for 45–55 minutes or until slightly browned on top.

Remove from the oven and allow to cool before serving.

Saveria Tip: Cannelloni are best left to rest for 15–20 minutes before serving. This will ensure the sauce is not too runny and has the perfect consistency.

lasagne ragu

layered pasta

Lasagne is always a loyal friend. It will not only feed an entire family, but will offer seconds as well as leftovers for meals during the week. Much thought, however, must go into the layering process. Although this dish looks simple to make, it can't be quickly thrown together. Follow the layering order and get lost in the technique. I find it quite therapeutic.

Serves 6

25–30 fresh lasagne sheets (see pasta all'uovo, pg. 44) **or 500 g** (1 lb 2 oz) **store-bought lasagne sheets**
8 cups ragu (pg. 42)
250 g (9 oz) **freshly grated mozzarella**
125 g (4½ oz) **freshly grated parmesan**
250 g (9 oz) **bacon, diced** (fat removed)
2 large eggs, beaten

Equipment:
baking tray, approximately 20 x 30cm (8 x 12 in.)

Directions:

Preheat the oven to 170°C (340°F).
If using fresh pasta, follow the steps for the pasta all'uovo recipe (pg. 44) until you roll the dough out to 1–2 mm thin, and it has rested for 30 minutes.

After the dough has rested, cut into lasagne sheets/shapes—10 x 15 cm (4 x 6 in) rectangles.

Start by cooking the lasagne sheets in boiling salted water until al dente (2–3 minutes for fresh pasta; 8–10 minutes for dry pasta).

Saveria Tip: To prevent the lasagne sheets from sticking together, place them in a criss-cross order when adding them to the water.

When the sheets are ready, transfer them directly to a bowl of cold water where they will stay until it's time to layer.

Begin the layering process in the baking tray. It is important to stick to the layering order:

1. Ragu sauce—cover all corners with a generous amount of sauce. (The ragu sauce must be smooth, so if there appears to be large pieces of meat, break them up with a fork.)

2. Lasagne sheets—leave no gaps.
3. Mozzarella
4. Parmesan
5. Bacon
6. Drizzle of beaten egg

Continue these steps until you fill the baking tray.

When you get to the top layer, use only ragu sauce, mozzarella and parmesan (no bacon or egg).

Cover the dish with foil, place in the oven and cook for 1 hour.

Remove from the oven and cool for 15 minutes before serving.

Crostoli

fried pastries

These charming fried pastries work really well with soft desserts to add crunch, but, honestly, I love them just the way they are.

Makes 50-60

3 large eggs
zest of 1 lemon, finely grated
1 tbsp. lemon juice
1 tbsp. olive oil
1 tsp. vanilla extract
pinch of salt
300 g (10½ oz / 2 cups) **plain** (all-purpose)
flour, sifted
vegetable oil, for frying
icing (confectioners') **sugar, to serve**

Equipment:
rolling pin
ravioli cutter

Directions:

In a bowl, combine the eggs, lemon zest, lemon juice, olive oil, vanilla extract and salt. Mix thoroughly.

Gradually sift in the flour, bit by bit, while mixing the ingredients together.

You should now have a dough that holds itself together and is not sticky. Rest the dough for 20 minutes.

Transfer the dough to a flat working surface lightly dusted with flour. Knead the dough for 5 minutes.

Roll out the mixture until very thin—about 1.5 mm.

Saveria Tip: Dust the top of your mixture with flour and wrap the edge of your dough around the rolling pin. Using your fingertips, apply a small amount of

pressure to the dough while simultaneously rolling the dough outwards along the stick. This will stretch it lengthways. Do this on each corner of the dough.

Using a ravioli cutter, cut the dough into crostoli strips—about 3.5 cm (1½ inches) wide and 8–10 cm (3¼–4 in) long.

Angle the edges of the strips for a classic crostoli shape. (Your crostoli should look like rectangles with crinkle-cut sides.)

Cut a slit in the middle of each shape.

Heat a large heavy-based frying pan one-quarter full of vegetable oil (enough for deep frying) over medium heat.

Test if the oil is hot enough by dropping a small amount of the mixture into the oil. If the mixture starts to fry immediately, the oil is ready.

Fry the crostoli in batches for 2–3 minutes on each side (using a slotted spoon to flip them over). They're ready when they begin to bubble and brown.

Use the slotted spoon to transfer the crostoli to paper towels to drain.

Cool completely for 20 minutes.

Once the crostoli are completely cooled, dust with icing sugar to finish.

Crostoli pastry is used when making cannoli. For the cannoli recipe, continue reading …

Cannoli

tubed custard pastries

Cannoli are the much-anticipated finale of the show, and we all appreciate them like no other dish—as Nonna dedicates a lot of time to crafting these delicacies. Enjoyed best with a strong cup of espresso, they're the ultimate Italian dessert.

Makes approximately 15

Crostoli ingredients (see pg. 52)

Custard:
1 litre (34 fl oz / 4 cups) **full-cream** (whole) **milk**
1 large egg yolk, beaten
1 tbsp. finely grated lemon zest
50 g (1¾ oz / ⅓ cup) **plain flour, sifted**
75 g (2¾ oz / ⅓ cup) **white sugar**
2 tbsp. cocoa powder

Equipment:
ravioli cutter, rolling pin, cannoli rollers, strainer

Pastry:

See the crostoli recipe (pg. 52) and follow the steps until your dough is rolled 1.5 mm thin.

Using the ravioli cutter, cut the dough into even squares about 7 cm (2¾ inches) across. Gently roll out each square with a rolling pin to further thin the dough. Roll each square (corner to corner) around a cannoli roller.

Seal the corners together using a mixture of flour and water, which will act as glue.

Heat a large heavy-based frying pan approximately one-quarter full of vegetable oil (enough for deep-frying) over medium heat.

Test if the oil is hot enough by dropping a small amount of the mixture into the oil. If the mixture starts to fry immediately, the oil is ready. When the oil is hot, fry the cannoli pastry (still around their rollers) in the oil until they bubble, brown and crisp (approximately 1–2 minutes). Make sure to turn the cannoli rollers while frying to brown all sides.

Use a slotted spoon to transfer the cannoli to paper towels to drain. Set aside and allow to cool.

Custard:

In a bowl, combine the milk, beaten egg yolk and lemon zest.

Gradually sift in the flour, bit by bit, while mixing the ingredients together.

Pour the mixture through a strainer to filter the lemon zest.

Saveria Tip: To break up the lumps of flour that may form, keep the strainer partly in the mixture and use a spoon to stir until all the flour is combined. Only the lemon zest should be left in the strainer.

Add the sugar to the mixture and stir to combine.

Pour the mixture into a medium-sized saucepan and cook over low heat, stirring constantly, in a clockwise motion, for approximately 10 minutes or until the mixture thickens to a custard.

Divide the mixture into two. Keep one half of the mixture as it is (lemon custard) and set aside in a bowl. Add the cocoa powder to the other half (chocolate custard), stir to combine and place back on the stove to cook for a few more minutes, stirring in a clockwise motion to combine the cocoa powder.

Let both custards cool completely.

Carefully remove the rollers from the cannoli pastry.

Using a spoon, scoop the custard into the cannoli, using the handle of a spoon to push it through the centre. Half-fill the pastry with lemon custard, then fill the rest with chocolate custard, right to the edge of the pastry.

Dust with sifted icing sugar.

Serve with a strong cup of espresso/caffé.

turdilli

honey balls

A very Calabrian sweet—and my sister's absolute favourite. These addictive dough balls are crafted exactly like gnocchi, then fried and completely covered in honey. I have fond memories of lying on Nonna's couch with my sister and a pile of what we call honey balls, watching the Italian channel while licking the honey off my fingers.

Serves 6

4 large eggs
good pinch of salt
300 g (10½ oz / 2 cups) **plain flour, sifted**
vegetable oil, for frying
350 g (12½ oz / 1 cup) **honey**

Directions:

In a bowl, whisk the eggs and salt for approximately 30 seconds.

Gradually sift the flour into the mixture while simultaneously mixing the ingredients together.
You should now have pliable dough.
Rest the dough for 20 minutes.

Transfer the dough to a lightly floured working surface and knead for 5 minutes.

Roll your mixture into thumb size logs, then cut into 2.5 cm (1 inch) pieces (exactly like gnocchi).

Shape the pieces. In one fast sharp movement, use your index finger to apply a small amount of pressure to the middle of each piece of dough while simultaneously rolling your finger down and off the pieces towards yourself. The result will be a small dint-like pocket in each piece of dough.

Heat a large heavy-based frying pan approximately one-quarter full of vegetable oil (enough for deep-frying) over medium heat.

Test if the oil is hot enough by dropping a small amount of the mixture into the oil. If the mixture starts to fry immediately, the oil is ready.

Fry the pieces of dough in batches, cooking until they puff and turn a dark golden brown (about 1 ½ minutes). Use a slotted spoon to transfer the pieces to paper towel to drain.

Warm the honey in a large saucepan over low heat for 30 seconds—this will soften the honey.
Stir continuously to prevent burning.

Add the fried dough pieces to the saucepan of honey and toss until they are all completely covered in honey.

Saveria Tip: It is important not to burn the honey as your turdilli will then taste like toffee—not what you're looking for.

Cool completely before serving.

Pile the turdilli on a serving plate. These are best eaten the same day, but can be stored in an airtight container and kept for 1 week.

turdilli di vino

wine balls

Turdilli di Vino—or honey balls with red wine—are the adult's version of Turdilli and are rich in flavour and completely indulgent. Now that I'm older, I have switched to enjoying Turdilli di Vino over Turdilli.

Makes 85-90

310 ml (10½ fl oz / 1¼ cups) **merlot wine**
190 ml (6½ fl oz / ¾ cup) **olive oil**
1 large egg, beaten
pinch of salt
525 g (1 lb 3 oz / 3½ cups) **plain flour, sifted**
vegetable oil for frying
350 g (12½ oz / 1 cup) **honey**

Directions:

In a large saucepan over medium heat, bring the wine and olive oil to the boil.

Take the pan off the heat and let the liquid cool for 5 minutes.

Add the egg and salt and stir to combine.

Gradually sift the flour into the mixture while mixing the ingredients together.

You should now have a dough that is not sticky and holds together. Rest the dough for 20 minutes.

Transfer the dough to a lightly floured working surface and knead for 5 minutes.

If, for some reason, your dough is still sticky and hard to work with, continue to knead through handfuls of flour until your dough is pliable.

Roll your mixture into thumb size logs, then cut into 5 cm (2 inch) long pieces (twice the size as honey balls and gnocchi).

Using your index finger and your middle finger, apply a small amount of pressure to the middle of each piece while simultaneously rolling your

finger down and off (towards yourself). The result will be a dint-like pocket on each piece.

Heat a large heavy-based frying pan approximately one-quarter full of vegetable oil (enough for deep-frying) over medium heat.

Test if the oil is hot enough by dropping a small amount of the mixture into the oil. If the mixture starts to fry immediately, the oil is ready.

Fry the pieces until they turn a dark purplish brown (approximately 3 minutes).
Stir every 20–30 seconds to prevent burning.

Warm the honey in a large saucepan over low heat for 30 seconds—this will soften the honey.
Stir continuously to prevent burning.

Add the now-fried pieces and toss until they are completely covered in honey.

Cool completely before serving.

Pile the turdilli di vino on a serving plate. These are best eaten the same day, but can be stored in an airtight container and kept for 1 week.

mutsasola

biscotti

When Saveria was young, she would make a simple biscotti with honey, flour and egg. On the boat over to Australia, she met a fellow traveller called Carmella, who always carried a pocket full of almonds. Saveria would cook biscotti for the passengers and, one day, Carmella asked, 'Why don't we add almonds?'
This recipe represents the longstanding friendship of Saveria and Carmella. Today you will still find tins and tins of fresh biscotti in Saveria's backroom, ready to give as parting gifts to all the cousins who regularly come to visit.

Makes 120 - 140

260 g (9 oz / ¾ cup) **honey**
½ beaten egg
235 g (8½ oz / 1½ cups) **almonds**
300 g (10½ oz / 2 cups) **plain flour**
1 tbsp. self-raising flour

Equipment:
1 large baking tray or 2 small baking trays

Preheat the oven to 170°C (340°F).

Pour water into a saucepan until it's one-third full, then bring it to a boil.

Place the honey in a large metal bowl and sit the bowl over the top of the saucepan. Warm the honey for 30 seconds to 1 minute, or until the honey turns to liquid. Make sure to stir continuously to prevent burning. Remove the bowl from the heat and let the honey cool for 5 minutes.

Add the beaten egg and half the portion of almonds to the honey. Mix thoroughly. Mix self-raising flour and plain flour together. Add small portions of the flour mixture while mixing the ingredients together. Continue this until the mixture begins to thicken.

Transfer the mixture to a lightly dusted working surface and use your hands to work the rest of the flour through. You should now have dough that holds together.

Add the remaining almonds to the dough and combine.

Knead the mixture for a few minutes until all ingredients are completely combined into an even dough.
If the mixture is too sticky to work with, add an extra handful of flour.

Cut the biscotti mixture in half and roll both portions into thick logs approximately 35 cm (1 ft 1½ in) long.

Using your fingertips, apply pressure to the surface of the logs, flattening them while keeping their edges rounded. (The shape should look like a rectangle with rounded edges.) The logs should be 7–8 cm (2¾–3¼ inches) wide and 5 mm (¼ inch) in thickness.

Saveria Tip: If you are cooking alone, it is important to cook the biscotti portions separately. This is because biscotti can only be cut when straight out of the oven. Biscotti hardens very quickly and becomes too hard to cut. If you cook both, by the time you finish cutting the first log, the second will be too hard to cut.

Place the biscotti logs on the large baking tray or two smaller ones and put in the oven. Cook for approximately 30 minutes (this may vary depending on your oven's strength) or until the mixture turns pale gold.

Turn the biscotti logs over and cook the bases for 5 more minutes.

Transfer from the oven to a flat working surface.

Using a sharp knife, cut the biscotti into 5 mm (¼ inch) thin biscotti slices.

Cool the biscotti for 20 minutes before serving.

These delicious biscuits are best served with a strong cup of espresso (just pop a few on everyone's saucer). Alternatively, serve on a gorgeous plate with a glass of Italian liqueur like limoncello, frangelico, anice or amaretto.

You can store these biscotti in an airtight container at room temperature. These will keep for several months.

love Saveria

pizzelle
wafer biscuits

Nonna would always give us a big bag of these biscuits when we were going on long trips to settle our stomachs. They're delicious just as they are, but if you use a cone tool when making them, they can be filled with gelati and sweets.

Makes approx. 18 large wafer shapes

4 large eggs, beaten
110 g (4 oz / ½ cup) **sugar**
100 ml olive oil
zest of 1 lemon, finely grated
225 g (8 oz / 1½ cups) **plain** (all-purpose) **flour**

Equipment:
electric mixer
pizzelle press
toothpick

Directions:

In an electric mixer, thoroughly combine the eggs and sugar for 2 minutes.

Add the oil and lemon zest to the mixture and combine.

Gradually add the flour to the mixture, handful by handful, while simultaneously combining the ingredients together.

Continue to mix until your batter is thick and holds its shape around a spoon.

Heat the pizzelle press on high (the iron must be very hot). Add a tablespoon at a time to the centre of the hot iron plates, then press down the lid.

Hold the lid down for approximately 30 seconds to 1 minute or until the biscuits are brown and crisp.

Saveria Tip: To prevent the biscuits from burning, lift the lid a few times during cooking to release the steam from the iron.

Using a toothpick, carefully remove the cookies from the iron by piercing each one and rapidly transferring to a plate (if your appliance has breaking grooves, break the biscuits appropriately).

Pizzelle are beautiful on their own. However, by using a cone tool, they can be made into waffle cones to be filled with ice cream and sweets. Simply roll the hot pizzelle around a cone-shaped mould after they come off the press and seal the ends together. Cool the pizzelle cones completely on the mould before removing them and filling with ice cream.

Buon appetito!

georgia Spanos